AN INVITATION TO FAITH

AN A TO Z PRIMER ON
THE THOUGHT OF POPE BENEDICT XVI

Edited by Jean-Michel Coulet

With an introduction by Cardinal Georges Cottier, O.P.

English translation supervised by Kate Marcelin-Rice

A Giniger Book
Published in association with
IGNATIUS PRESS   SAN FRANCISCO

Title of the French original:
L'Essence de la foi
© 2006 by Éditions Plon, Paris

This translation is published by arrangement with
The K. S. Giniger Company, Inc., New York

Cover photography by Stefano Spaziani

Cover design by Riz Boncan Marsella

The words of Pope Benedict XVI
© 2007 Libreria Editrice Vaticana
© 2007 by The K. S. Giniger Company
All rights reserved
ISBN 978-1-58617-213-8
Library of Congress Control Number 2007921430
Printed in the United States of America ∞

Dear English-speaking pilgrims,
may the healing power of Christ transform your lives and
fill you with his peace!

May you [be strengthened in]
your love of the Universal Church and
deepen your commitment to witness to
the "Good News" of Jesus Christ.

As we strive to follow closely the teachings of Jesus,
may our faith guide our steps
and give joy to our hearts.

I pray that by the intercession of the Blessed Lady,
you will grow ever closer to her Son Jesus Christ
and share his Good News
with all those you encounter.

May the light of Christ
shine ever more brightly and strongly in your lives!

Introduction

"I believe, we believe". This formulation, which in the *Catechism of the Catholic Church* introduces the commentary on the *profession of faith*, brings us to an awareness of the dual polarity of the theological faith.

"I believe". Adherence to the Word of God is a commitment of the whole person, called up from the depths of his freedom. It is the response to a vocation that is unique because its source is divine love, and love is a choice.

"We believe". This is how we profess the ecclesial dimension of the faith. The faith of each individual is the faith of the Church. This is one of the most beautiful aspects of the Christian identity. The personal dimension in no way signifies withdrawal into privacy, nor does the ecclesial dimension mean absorption into the collective. Adult faith is recognized by this: progress in interior devotion and progress in communion go hand in hand; they feed on each other.

This work, therefore, *An Invitation to Faith*, dedicated as it is to the words spoken by Pope Benedict XVI since the beginning of his Pontificate, invites us to nurture this faith and to go back to its source, which makes us say: "I believe, we believe".

Cardinal Georges Cottier, O.P.

Theologian Emeritus of the Pontifical Household

Foreword

"*Cooperatores veritatis*" (collaborators in truth) is the motto of Pope Joseph Ratzinger, who chose the name Benedict when he was elected to the Chair of Peter on April 19, 2005. Each of Peter's successors is vested with the *olim* and the *nunc*: on the one hand, a faithful continuity with the work of his immediate predecessors and the two-thousand-year-old tradition of the Church; on the other, the exercise of the Petrine ministry with unique sensitivity and keen attention to the signs of the times. In the footsteps of John Paul II and in fidelity to Saint Augustine, his master in thought, he became the tireless pilgrim of the Truth to be shared, to be taught, to be explained and to be discovered.

Benedict XVI immediately challenged the relativism of our times, which rejects God, sees nothing as definitive and, according to him, sets as the ultimate yardstick the individual's own ego and desires. The Pope offers instead an opposing standard: Christ, the Son of God, the true man. His words are rousing and demand an examination of conscience. His words are for all. He says: "An 'adult' faith is not a faith that follows the trends of fashion or the latest novelty; a mature and adult faith is deeply rooted in friendship with Christ. It is this friendship that opens us up to all that is good and that gives us the criterion by which to distinguish the true from the false, and deceit from truth." With strong words, Benedict XVI invites us to place God at the center of our lives. This book, *An Invitation to Faith*, is a selection of key words from the teachings of the Holy Father, presented in alphabetical order. Benedict XVI invites us to become daily actors in the real revolution that comes from God and is called Love.

Jean-Michel Coulet
Editor of the French-language edition
of *L'Osservatore Romano*

A

ANTHROPOLOGY
—*What is man?*

It must be forcefully stated that man cannot and must not ever be sacrificed to the success of science and technology: this is why the so-called "anthropological question" assumes its full importance. For us, the heirs of the humanist tradition founded on Christian values, this question should be faced in the light of the inspiring principles of our civilization.

The basic question today, as in the past, remains the anthropological question: What is man? From where does he come? Where must he go? How must he go? In other words, it is a matter of clarifying the conception of the human being on which new projects are based. And you are rightly asking yourselves which human being, which image of man, does the university intend to serve: an individual withdrawn into the defense of his own interests, a single perspective of interests, a materialistic perspective, or a person who is open to solidarity with others in the search for the true meaning of existence, which must be a common meaning that transcends the individual?

ATHEISM

—Lack of guidance?

HOW MANY people today are deceived by atheism, and seek to prove that it is scientific to think that all things lack guidance and order!

B

BAPTISM:
—A community of friends

THROUGH Baptism each child is inserted into a gathering of friends who never abandon him in life or in death, because these companions are God's family, which in itself bears the promise of eternity.

BENEDICT
—Saint Benedict, the search for God

BENEDICT pointed out to his followers the search for God as the fundamental and, indeed, the one and only aim of life: "*Quaerere Deum*". He knew, however, that when the believer enters into a profound relationship with God, he cannot be content with a mediocre life under the banner of a minimalistic ethic and a superficial religiosity. In this light one can understand better the expression that Benedict borrowed from Saint Cyprian and summed up in his Rule (IV, 21), the monks' program of life: "*Nihil amori Christi praeponere*", "Let nothing be preferred to the love of Christ." Holiness consists in this, a sound proposal for every Christian that has become a real and urgent pastoral need in our time, when we feel the need to anchor life and history to sound spiritual references.

C

CHARITY
—*Love in practice*

CHRISTIAN charity is first of all the simple response to immediate needs and specific situations: feeding the hungry, clothing the naked, caring for and healing the sick, visiting those in prison, etc.

⁂

Christian charitable activity must be independent of parties and ideologies. It is not a means of changing the world ideologically, and it is not at the service of worldly stratagems, but it is a way of making present here and now the love which man always needs.

CHURCH AND SOCIETY
—*The Church, a factor of unity*

IN MANY developing countries, I have also seen how the Church with her Catholic unity is the great factor that unites in dispersion. In many situations, the Church has remained the one reality that functions and makes life continue, that provides the necessary assistance, guarantees coexistence and helps to find the possibility of creating one great solution. In this sense, in these situations, the Church also carries out a service that replaces the political level, giving the possibility of living together and of rebuilding communion after destruction and of rebuilding, after the outburst of hatred, the spirit of reconciliation.

COMMANDMENTS
—The way of freedom

AT A CLOSER look, the Commandments are the means that the Lord gives us to protect our freedom, both from the internal conditioning of passions and from the external abuse of those with evil intentions. The "noes" of the Commandments are as many "yeses" to the growth of true freedom.

COVENANT
—A presence that unites

PENTECOST is a new Sinai, the *feast of the New Covenant*, where the Covenant with Israel is extended to all the nations of the earth. The Church has been catholic and missionary from her birth. The universality of salvation is meaningfully manifested with the list of the numerous ethnic groups to which those who heard the Apostles' first proclamation belonged. The People of God, which had found its first configuration in Sinai, extends today to the point of surmounting every barrier of race, culture, space and time. As opposed to what occurred with the tower of Babel, when people wanted to build a way to Heaven with their hands and ended up by destroying their very capacity for mutual understanding, in Pentecost the Spirit, with the gift of tongues, demonstrates that his presence unites and transforms confusion into communion.

CULTURE
—*The danger of secularization*

IT IS possible to identify two basic lines of our current secularized society that are clearly interdependent. They impel people to move away from the Christian proclamation and cannot but have an effect on those whose inclinations and choices of life are developing. One of these is agnosticism, which derives from the reduction of human intelligence to a mere practical mechanism that tends to stifle the religious sense engraved in the depths of our nature. The other is the process of relativization and uprooting, which corrodes the most sacred bonds and most worthy affections of the human being, with the result that people are debilitated and our reciprocal relations rendered precarious and unstable.

CULTURE
—The right to education

IT IS of the utmost importance to mobilize the energies of intelligence so that the human person's right to education and culture may be recognized everywhere, particularly in the poorest countries.

D

DEATH

—Falling into God's hands

THIS WORLD of ours is a world of fear: the fear of misery and poverty, the fear of illness and suffering, the fear of solitude, the fear of death. We have in this world a widely developed insurance system; it is good that it exists. But we know that at the moment of deep suffering, at the moment of the ultimate loneliness of death, no insurance policy will be able to protect us. The only valid insurance in those moments is the one that comes to us from the Lord, who also assures us: "Do not fear, I am always with you." We can fall, but in the end we fall into God's hands, and God's hands are good hands.

DIALOGUE

—The dialogue between religions, reception and reciprocity

THE CATHOLIC CHURCH realizes with increasing awareness that interreligious dialogue is part of her commitment to the service of humanity in the contemporary world. This conviction has become, as one says, "daily bread" especially fit for those who work in contact with migrants, refugees and with different categories of itinerant people. We are living in times in which Christians are called to cultivate a style of dialogue open to the religious question, without failing to present to the interlocutors the Christian proposal consistent with her own identity.

In its action of reception and dialogue with migrants and itinerant peoples, the Christian community has as its constant reference point Christ, who left to his disciples, as a rule of life, the new commandment of love. Christian love is, by its nature, prevenient. This is why the individual believer is called to open his arms and his heart to every person, from whatever nation he comes, allowing the authorities responsible for public life to enforce the relevant laws held to be appropriate for a healthy coexistence.

One increasingly feels the importance of reciprocity in dialogue, reciprocity defined as a "principle" of great importance. It treats of a "relationship based on mutual respect", and before that, on an "attitude of heart and spirit". The importance and delicacy of this commitment are witnessed by the efforts made in many communities to weave with immigrants relations of mutual awareness and esteem, which appear ever more useful to overcome prejudice and a closed mentality.

E

EUCHARIST
—Nourished by Christ

ADORATION means entering the depths of our hearts in communion with the Lord, who makes himself bodily present in the Eucharist. In the monstrance, he always entrusts himself to us and asks us to be united with his Presence, with his risen Body.

Anyone nourished with the faith of Christ at the Eucharistic Table assimilates his same style of life, which is the style of service especially attentive to the weakest and most underprivileged persons.

EXPERIENCE, PERSONAL
—My vocation to serving God

MY VOCATION to the priesthood grew with me, almost naturally, without any dramatic events of conversion. Two other things also helped me on this journey: already as a boy, helped by my parents and by the parish priest, I had discovered the beauty of the Liturgy, and I came to love it more and more because I felt that divine beauty appears in it and that Heaven unfolds before us. The second element was the discovery of the beauty of knowledge, of knowing God and Sacred Scripture, thanks to which it is possible to enter into that great adventure of dialogue with God which is theology. Thus, it was a joy to enter into this thousand-year-old work of theology, this celebration of the Liturgy in which God is with us and celebrates with us.

F

FAITH
—*The bond that unites us*

THE CREED is always a shared act; it means letting ourselves be incorporated into a communion of progress, life, words and thought. We do not "have" faith, in the sense that it is primarily God who gives it to us. Nor do we "have" it, either, in the sense that it must not be invented by us. We must let ourselves fall, so to speak, into the communion of faith, of the Church. Believing is in itself a Catholic act. It is participation in this great certainty, which is present in the Church as a living subject.

A faith lived in depth, which is fully open to today but also fully open to God, combines two things: respect for otherness and newness and the continuity of our being, communicability between people and between times.

Christianity precisely emphasizes history and religion as a historical event, an event in history starting with Abraham. Then as a historical faith, after opening the door to modernity with its sense of progress and by constantly moving ahead, Christianity is at the same time a faith based on the Creator who reveals himself and makes himself present in a history to which he gives continuity, hence communicability between souls. A faith lived in depth, which is fully open to today but also fully open to God, combines the two things: respect for otherness and newness and the continuity of our being, communicability between people and between times.

FAMILY
—The family, the foundation of society

THE CHURCH sees in the family a most important value that must be defended from any attack that aims to undermine its solidity and call its very existence into question.

⁊⁊⁊

It is all the more necessary for us as a Church to help families, which are the fundamental cell of every healthy society. Only in families, therefore, is it possible to create a communion of generations in which the memory of the past lives on in the present and is open to the future. Thus, life truly continues and progresses. Real progress is impossible without this continuity of life, and once again, it is impossible without the religious element. Without trust in God, without trust in Christ, who in addition gives us the ability to believe and to live, the family cannot survive. We see this today. Only faith in Christ and only sharing the faith of the Church saves the family; and on the other hand, only if the family is saved can the Church also survive.

FEAR OF THE LORD
—The source of wisdom

CULTIVATE "fear of the Lord", the beginning of true wisdom. It is not fear and terror that are suggested by this word, but a serious and sincere respect that is the fruit of love, a genuine and active attachment to God the Liberator.

The voice of one of the faithful joins that of the whole community, expresses the hope that the

Lord will open his hands to lavish his gifts of justice and freedom upon us. The faithful are in need of God's intervention because they are in a painful plight, suffering the contempt and disdain of overbearing people. The righteous have entrusted their cause to the Lord; he is not indifferent to their beseeching eyes, nor does he ignore their plea—and ours—or disappoint their hope.

FORGIVENESS AND PEACE
—Elements of peace

ASKING for forgiveness and granting forgiveness—which is likewise an obligation, since everyone is included in the Lord's admonition: *"Let whoever is without sin cast the first stone!"*—are indispensable elements for peace.

FREEDOM
—Setting freedom free

IT IS not easy to recognize and find authentic happiness in this world in which we live, where people are often held captive by the current ways of thinking. They may think they are "free", but they are being led astray and become lost amid the errors or illusions of aberrant ideologies. "Freedom itself needs to be set free", and the darkness in which mankind is groping needs to be illuminated. Jesus taught us how this can be done: "If you continue in my word, you are truly my disciples; and you will know the truth, and the truth will make you free." The incarnate Word, Word of Truth, makes us free and directs our freedom toward the good.

FRIENDSHIP WITH JESUS
—*The Lord will never abandon me*

FRIENDSHIP with the Teacher guarantees profound peace and serenity to the soul even in the dark moments and in the most arduous trials. When faith meets with dark nights, in which the presence of God is no longer "felt" or "seen", friendship with Jesus guarantees that in reality nothing can ever separate us from his love.

It is important to be attentive to the Lord's gestures on our journey. He speaks to us through events, through people, through encounters: it is necessary to be attentive to all of this.

Then, a second point: it is necessary to enter into real friendship with Jesus in a personal relationship with him and not to know who Jesus is only from others or from books, but to live an ever deeper personal relationship with Jesus, where we can begin to understand what he is asking of us.

And then, the awareness of what I am, of my possibilities: on the one hand, courage, and on the other, humility, trust and openness, with the help of friends, of Church authority and also of priests, of families: What does the Lord want of me? Of course, this is always a great adventure, but life can be successful only if we have the courage to be adventurous, trusting that the Lord will never leave me alone, that the Lord will go with me and help me.

G

GENERATIONS
—The discovery of faith

DISCOVERING the beauty and joy of faith is a path that every new generation must take on its own, for all that we have that is most our own and most intimate is staked on faith: our heart, our mind, our freedom, in a deeply personal relationship with the Lord at work within us.

GOD
—The Word of Life

CAN WE love God without seeing him?

While we are on this earth, our relationship with God takes place more by listening than by seeing; and the same contemplation comes about, so to speak, with closed eyes, thanks to the interior light that is kindled in us by the Word of God.

A Christian knows when it is time to speak of God and when it is better to say nothing and to let love alone speak. He knows that God is love and that God's presence is felt at the very time when the only thing we do is to love.

⁓

The Word of God carries life within it! And it bears fruit! The Parable also says that much of the seed did not bear fruit because it fell on the path, on patches of rock and so forth. But the part that fell on the rich soil bore a yield of thirty- or sixty- or a hundredfold. This enables us to understand that we too must be courageous, even if the Word of God, the Kingdom of God, seems to have no historical or political importance. In the end, Jesus made people realize that he himself was the grain of wheat that fell into the earth and died. In the Crucifixion, everything seems to have failed, but precisely in this way, falling into the earth and dying, on the Way of the Cross, it bore fruit for each epoch, for every epoch. We learn from the Word of the Lord that this seed alone transforms the earth ever anew and opens it to true life.

⁓

The world cannot live without God, the God of Revelation—and not just any God: we see how dangerous a cruel God, an untrue God can be—the God who showed us his Face in Jesus Christ.

This Face of the One who suffered for us, this loving Face of the One who transforms the world. Therefore, we ourselves have this very deep certainty that Christ is the answer and that without the concrete God, the God with the Face of Christ, the world destroys itself.

***

A liar loses his sense of the supreme truth, of God. In this way, he becomes hard of heart and incapable of conversion. Today, the Lord alerts us to the self-sufficiency that puts a limit on his unlimited love. He invites us to imitate his humility, to entrust ourselves to it, to let ourselves be "infected" by it. He invites us—however lost we may feel—to return home, to let his purifying goodness uplift us and enable us to sit at table with him, with God himself.

***

We all ask ourselves what the Lord expects of us. It seems to me that the great challenge of our time is secularization: that is, a way of living and presenting the world as if *"Deus non daretur"*, in other words, as if God did not exist. There is a desire to reduce God to the private sphere, to a sentiment, as if he were not an objective reality. As a result, everyone makes his own plan of life. But this vision, presented as though it were scientific, accepts as valid only what can be proven. With a God who is not available for immediate experimentation, this vision ends by also injuring society. The result is in fact that each one makes his own plan and in the end finds himself opposed to the other. As can be seen, this is definitely an unlivable situation. We must make God present again in our society. This seems to me to be the first essential element: that God be once again present in our lives, that we do not live as though we were autonomous, authorized to invent what freedom and life are.

God exists or he does not exist. There are only two options. Either one recognizes the priority of reason, of creative Reason, which is at the beginning of all things and is the principle of all things—the priority of reason is also the priority of freedom—or one holds the priority of the irrational, inasmuch as everything that functions on our earth and

33

in our lives would be only accidental, marginal, an irrational result—reason would be a product of irrationality. One cannot ultimately "prove" either project, but the great option of Christianity is the option for rationality and for the priority of reason. This seems to me to be an excellent option, which shows us that behind everything is a great Intelligence to which we can entrust ourselves.

"You are clean, but not all of you", the Lord says. This sentence reveals the great gift of purification that he offers to us, because he wants to be at table together with us, to become our food. "But not all of you"—the obscure mystery of rejection exists, which becomes apparent with Judas' act, and precisely on Holy Thursday, the day on which Jesus made the gift of himself, it should give us food for thought. The Lord's love knows no bounds, but man can put a limit on it.

To respond to God's call and set out, it is not necessary to be perfect already. We know that the Prodigal Son's awareness of his sin enabled him to start out on the path of return and thereby to experience the joy of reconciliation with the

Father. Human limitations and fragility are not an obstacle, on condition that they help to make us ever more aware that we need Christ's redeeming love.

GRACE

—A river that flows through history

THE ENTIRE Church, as beloved Pope John Paul II used to say, is one great movement animated by the Holy Spirit, a river that flows through history to irrigate it with God's grace and make it full of life, goodness, beauty, justice and peace.

Grace is the power that transforms man and the world; *peace* is the mature fruit of this transformation. Christ is grace; Christ is peace.

The grace that the Father gives us in his Only-begotten Son is therefore the manifestation of his love that enfolds and transforms us. The divine grace was "freely bestowed" upon us. We thus penetrate the infinite and glorious depths of God's mystery, opened and revealed through grace to whoever is called by grace and by love, since it is impossible to arrive at this revelation endowed with human intelligence and ability alone.

H

HUMANITY
—*The route of humanity*

In the mirror of the Cross we have seen all the sufferings of humanity today. In the Cross of Christ we have seen the suffering of abandoned and abused children; the threats to the family; the division of the world into the pride of the rich who do not see Lazarus at the door and the misery of the multitudes who are suffering hunger and thirst. But we have also seen "stations" of consolation. We have seen the Mother, whose goodness stays faithful unto death and beyond death. We have seen the courageous woman, who stood before the Lord and was not afraid to show solidarity with this Suffering One. We have seen Simon the Cyrenian, an African, who carried the Cross with Jesus. Finally, we have seen, through these "stations" of consolation, that consolation, like suffering, is neverending. We have seen that on the Way of the Cross, Paul found the zeal of his faith and kindled the light of love. We have seen how Saint Augustine found his way: as well as Francis of Assisi, Saint

Vincent de Paul, Saint Maximilian Kolbe and Mother Teresa of Calcutta. So it is that we too are invited to find our place, to discover with these great, courageous saints the way with Jesus and for Jesus: the way of goodness and truth; the courage of love.

I

INDIFFERENCE

—*May the breath of the Spirit blow on earth*

HUMAN PRIDE and egoism always create divisions, build walls of indifference, hate and violence. The Holy Spirit, on the other hand, makes hearts capable of understanding the languages of all, as he re-establishes the bridge of authentic communion between earth and Heaven.

J

JESUS
—*The way of perfection*

JESUS CHRIST is the way of perfection, the living and personal synthesis of perfect freedom in total obedience to God's will.

~~~~~~~

Jesus is the Pole Star of human freedom: without him it loses its sense of direction, for without the knowledge of the truth, freedom degenerates, becomes isolated and is reduced to sterile arbitration. With him, freedom is rediscovered; it is recognized to have been created for our good and is expressed in charitable actions and behavior.

JOSEPH
—*The way of humility*

THE FIGURE of this great Saint, even though remaining somewhat hidden, is of fundamental importance in the history of salvation. Above all, as part of the tribe of Judah, he united Jesus to the Davidic lineage so that, fulfilling the promises regarding the Messiah, the Son of the Virgin Mary may truly be called the "Son of David". The Gospel of Matthew highlights in a special way the Messianic prophecies that reached fulfillment through the role Joseph played: the birth of Jesus in Bethlehem; his journey through Egypt, where the Holy Family took refuge; the nickname, the "Nazarene". In all of this he showed himself, like his spouse, Mary, an authentic heir of Abraham's faith: faith in God who guides the events of history according to his mysterious salvific plan. His greatness, like Mary's, stands out even more because his mission was carried out in the humility and hiddenness of the house of Nazareth. Moreover, God himself, in the person of his Incarnate Son, chose this way and style of life—humility and hiddenness—in his earthly existence.

From the example of Saint Joseph we all receive a strong invitation to carry out with fidelity, simplicity and modesty the task that Providence has entrusted to us. I think especially of fathers and mothers of families, and I pray that they will always be able to appreciate the beauty of a simple and industrious life, cultivating the conjugal relationship with care and fulfilling with enthusiasm the great and difficult educational mission.

JUSTICE
—Working for a just order

CHRISTIANS are called to seek justice always but to possess an inner impulse to love that goes beyond justice itself.

In recent times, it has become clearer to all of us that justice and charity are the two inseparable aspects of the single social commitment of Christians. It is incumbent on lay faithful in particular to work for a just order in society, taking part in public life in the first person, cooperating with other citizens and fulfilling their own responsibility.

L

LAW OF GOD
—A gift of God

THERE is no contradiction between God's law and human freedom: God's law correctly interpreted neither attenuates nor, even less, eliminates man's freedom. On the contrary, it guarantees and fosters this freedom because "freedom attains its perfection when directed toward God, our beatitude."

By the Law that he gave through Moses, the Lord revealed that he wanted to make a covenant with Israel. The Law, therefore, is a gift more than an imposition. Rather than commanding what the human being ought to do, its intention is to reveal to all the choice of God: He takes the side of the Chosen People; he set them free from slavery and surrounds them with his merciful goodness.

LIFE
—Choosing life

MOSES' great discourse, on the threshold of the Holy Land after the forty-year pilgrimage in the

43

desert, sums up the whole of the Torah, the whole of the Law. Here we find the essential, not only for the Jewish people but also for us. This essential is the Word of God: "I have set before you life and death, blessing and curse; therefore, choose life." These fundamental words of Lent are also the fundamental words of the legacy of our great Pope John Paul II: "Choose life." This is our priestly vocation: to choose life ourselves and to help others to choose life.

~~~~~

The protection of life in all its stages, from the first moment of conception until natural death, the recognition and promotion of the natural structure of the family—as a union between a man and a woman based on marriage—the protection of the right of parents to educate their children are principles that are not truths of faith, even though they receive further light and confirmation from faith; they are inscribed in human nature itself, and therefore they are common to all humanity.

~~~~~

We all know that to reach a goal in a sport or in one's profession, discipline and sacrifices are required; but then, by reaching a desired goal, it is all crowned with success. Life itself is like this. In other words, becoming men and women according to Jesus' plan demands sacrifices, but these are by no means negative; on the contrary, they are a help in living as people with new hearts, in living a truly human and happy life. Since a consumer culture exists that wants to prevent us from living in accordance with the Creator's plan, we must have the courage to create islands, oases, and then great stretches of land of Catholic culture where the Creator's design is lived out.

LOVE

—God's passionate love for man

WE HAVE come to believe in God's love: in these words the Christian can express the fundamental decision of his life. Being Christian is not the result of an ethical choice or a lofty idea, but the encounter with an event, a person, which gives life a new horizon and a decisive direction.

God's love for us is fundamental for our lives, and it raises important questions about who God is and who we are.

God's passionate love for his people—for humanity—is at the same time a forgiving love. It is so great that it turns God against himself, his love against his justice. Here Christians can see a dim prefigurement of the mystery of the Cross: so great is God's love for man that by becoming man he follows him even into death, and so reconciles justice and love.

Amid this multiplicity of meanings [of *love*], one in particular stands out: love between man and woman, where body and soul are inseparably joined and human beings glimpse an apparently irresistible promise of happiness. This would seem to be the very epitome of love; all other kinds of love immediately seem to fade in comparison.

"God is love." It is there that this truth can be contemplated. It is from there that our definition of love must begin. In this contemplation the Christian discovers the path along which his life and love must move.

Eros tends to rise "in ecstasy" toward the Divine, to lead us beyond ourselves; yet for this very reason it calls for a path of ascent, renunciation, purification and healing.

Love is indeed "ecstasy", not in the sense of a moment of intoxication, but rather as a journey, an ongoing exodus out of the closed inward-looking self towards its liberation through self-giving, and thus towards authentic self-discovery and indeed the discovery of God.

Eros needs to be disciplined and purified if it is to provide, not just fleeting pleasure, but a certain foretaste of the pinnacle of our existence, of that beatitude for which our whole being yearns.

Since God has first loved us, love is now no longer a mere "command"; it is the response to the gift of love with which God draws near to us.

Love and truth are sources of life, are life itself.

Can we love God without seeing him?

Everything in this world will pass away. In eternity only Love will remain.

Love alone enables us to live, and love is always also suffering: it matures in suffering and provides the strength to suffer for good without taking oneself into account at the actual moment.

God used the way of love to reveal the intimate mystery of his Trinitarian life.

Love is "divine" because it comes from God and unites us to God; through this unifying process it makes us a "we" which transcends our divisions and makes us one, until in the end God is "all in all".

Love is never "finished" and complete; throughout life, it changes and matures and thus remains faithful to itself.

M

MARRIAGE
—God's plan

MARRIAGE is this following of the other in love, thus becoming one existence, one flesh, therefore inseparable; a new life that is born from this communion of love that unites and thus also creates the future. Medieval theologians, interpreting this affirmation which is found at the beginning of Sacred Scripture, said that marriage is the first of the seven sacraments to have been instituted by God already at the moment of creation, in Paradise, at the beginning of history and before any human history.

It is only the rock of total, irrevocable love between a man and a woman that can serve as the foundation on which to build a society that will become a home for all mankind.

The various forms of the erosion of marriage, such as free unions and "trial marriage", and even pseudo-marriages between people of the same sex, are instead expressions of an anarchic freedom that is wrongly made to pass as true human liberation.

Marriage and the family are rooted in the inmost nucleus of the truth about man and his destiny.

No people can ignore the precious good of the family, founded on marriage.

The matrimonial covenant, by which a man and a woman establish between themselves a partnership of the whole of life, is by its nature ordered toward the good of the spouses and the procreation and education of offspring: this is the foundation of the family and the patrimony and common good of humanity. Thus, the Church cannot cease to proclaim that in accordance with God's plans marriage and the family are irreplaceable and permit no other alternatives.

Man has always known, in a certain sense, that other forms of relationship between a man and a woman do not truly correspond with the original design for his being. And thus, in cultures, especially in the great cultures, we see again and again how they are oriented to this reality: monogamy, the man and the woman becoming one flesh. This is how a new generation can grow in fidelity, how a cultural tradition can endure, renew itself in continuity and make authentic progress.

The close relationship that exists between the image of God-Love and human love enables us to understand that: corresponding to the image of a monotheistic God is monogamous marriage.

The sacrament of marriage is not an invention of the Church; it is really "con-created" with man as such, as a fruit of the dynamism of love in which the man and the woman find themselves and thus also find the Creator who called them to love.

MARTYRDOM
—*The high price to pay for faith professed*

How can we not recognize that professing the Christian faith demands the heroism of the Martyrs in our time, too, in various parts of the world? Moreover, how can we not say that everywhere, even where there is no persecution, there is a high price to pay for consistently living the Gospel?

MARY
—*"Beloved" of God*

Mary is a woman who loves. How could it be otherwise? As a believer who in faith thinks with God's thoughts and wills with God's will, she cannot fail to be a woman who loves.

⁕

Mary's greatness consists in the fact that she wants to magnify God, not herself.

⁕

Saint Augustine imagines a dialogue between himself and the Angel of the Annunciation, in which he asks: "Tell me, O Angel, why did this happen in Mary?" The answer, says the Messenger, is contained in the very words of the greeting: "Hail, full of grace" (cf. *Sermo* 291:6).

In fact, the Angel, "appearing to her", does not call her by her earthly name, Mary, but by her divine name, as she has always been seen and characterized by God: "Full of grace—*gratia plena*", "full of grace", and the grace is none other than the love of God; thus, in the end, we can translate this word: "beloved" of God. Mary is the perfect disciple of her Son, who realizes the fullness of his freedom and thus exercises the freedom through obedience to the Father.

MEDIA
—Forming minds

TODAY, the mass media have a special role in the world of culture. It is known that not only do they inform people, but they also form the minds of those they address. They can therefore be an invaluable means of evangelization. People of the Church, especially lay Christians, are called to promote Gospel values in an even greater outreach through the press, radio, television and Internet.

MERCY

—God's "weapon"

The power that imposes a limit on evil is Divine Mercy. Violence, the display of evil, is opposed in history—as "the totally other" of God, God's own power—by Divine Mercy. The Lamb is stronger than the dragon, we could say together with the Book of Revelation.

N

NATURAL LAW
—A compass

THE CREATOR, because we are creatures, has inscribed his "natural law", a reflection of his creative idea, in our hearts, in our very being, as a compass and inner guide for our life. For this very reason, Sacred Scripture, Tradition and the Magisterium of the Church tell us that the vocation and complete fulfillment of the human being are attained, not by rejecting God's law, but by abiding by the new law.

NEIGHBOR
—The one I can help

ANYONE who needs me, and whom I can help, is my neighbor.

OPTION

—The option of a "yes" to life

THE CHRISTIAN option is basically very simple: it is the option to say "yes" to life. But this "yes" takes place only with a God who is known, with a God with a human face. It takes place by following this God in the communion of love.

P

PEACE
—*The courage of peace*

TODAY TOO, there is a need to convert to God, to God who is Love, so that the world may be freed from war and terrorism.

※

When man allows himself to be enlightened by the splendor of truth, he inwardly becomes a courageous peacemaker.

※

God, who is perfect and subsisting Love, has revealed himself in Jesus, embracing our human condition. In this way he has also pointed out to us the way of peace: dialogue, forgiveness, solidarity. This is the only path that leads to true peace.

※

In the face of the lasting situations of injustice and violence that continue to oppress various parts of the earth, in the face of those that are emerging as new and more insidious threats to peace—terrorism, nihilism and fanatical fundamentalism—it is becoming more necessary than ever to work together for peace! A "start" of courage and trust in God and man is necessary if we are to choose the path of peace.

Man is capable of knowing the truth! He has this capacity with regard to the great problems of being and acting: individually and as a member of society, whether of a single nation or of humanity as a whole.

If peace is the aspiration of every person of good will, for Christ's disciples it is a permanent mandate that involves all; it is a demanding mission that impels them to announce and witness to "the Gospel of Peace", proclaiming that recognition of God's full truth is an indispensable pre-condition for the consolidation of the truth of peace. May this awareness continue to grow so that every Christian community becomes the "leaven" of a humanity renewed by love.

PRAYER

—The power of prayer

THE CHRISTIAN who prays seeks an encounter with the Father of Jesus Christ, asking God to be present with the consolation of the Spirit to him and his work.

The person of prayer has the feeling that he lies on a beach, miraculously saved from the pounding fury of the waves. Human life is surrounded by the snares of evil lying in wait that not only attack the person's life but also aim at destroying all human values. However, the Lord rises to preserve the just and save him.

Prayer, as a means of drawing ever new strength from Christ, is concretely and urgently needed. People who pray are not wasting their time, even though the situation appears desperate and seems to call for action alone. Piety does not undermine the struggle against the poverty of our neighbors, however extreme.

Q

QUEENSHIP

*—Queen of Heaven and earth,
she is always close to us*

MARY is taken up body and soul into the glory of Heaven, and with God and in God she is Queen of Heaven and earth. And is she really so remote from us?

The contrary is true. Precisely because she is with God and in God, she is very close to each one of us.

While she lived on this earth she could be close to only a few people. Being in God, who is close to us, actually, "within" all of us, Mary shares in this closeness of God. Being in God and with God, she is close to each one of us, knows our hearts, can hear our prayers, can help us with her motherly kindness and has been given to us, as the Lord said, precisely as a "mother" to whom we can turn at every moment.

She always listens to us, she is always close to us and, being Mother of the Son, participates in the power of the Son and in his goodness. We can always entrust our whole lives to this Mother, who is not far from any one of us.

In his [John Paul II's] spirituality and in his tireless ministry, the presence of Mary as Mother and Queen of the Church was made manifest to the eyes of all.

R

REASON
—*The priority of reason*

THE TRUE PROBLEM challenging faith today seems
to me to be the evil in the world: we ask ourselves
how it can be compatible with the Creator's rationality. And here we truly need God, who was made
flesh and shows us that he is not only a mathemati-
cal reason but that this original Reason is also Love.
If we look at the great options, the Christian option today is the one that is the most rational and
the most human. Therefore, we can confidently
work out a philosophy, a vision of the world based
on this priority of reason, on this trust that the
creating Reason is love and that this love is God.

REFUSAL
—*Is God absent?*

OFTEN we cannot understand why God refrains
from intervening. Yet he does not prevent us from
crying out, like Jesus on the Cross: "My God, my

God, why have you forsaken me?" We should continue asking this question in prayerful dialogue before his face: "Lord, holy and true, how long will it be?"

RELATIVISM
—*The illusion of freedom*

TODAY, a particularly insidious obstacle to the task of educating is the massive presence in our society and culture of that relativism which, recognizing nothing as definitive, leaves as the ultimate criterion only the self with its desires. And under the semblance of freedom it becomes a prison for each one, for it separates people from one another, locking each person into his own "ego". With such a relativistic horizon, therefore, real education is not possible without the light of the truth; sooner or later, every person is in fact condemned to doubting in the goodness of his own life and the relationships of which it consists, the validity of his commitment to build with others something in common.

Today, in fact, a culture marked by individualistic relativism and positivist scientism is continuing to gain ground. It is a culture, therefore, that is tendentially closed to God and to his moral law, even if not always prejudicially opposed to Christianity. A great effort is therefore asked of Catholics to increase dialogue with the contemporary culture in order to open it to the perennial values of Transcendence.

S

SACRED SCRIPTURE
—The Lord speaks to us

THROUGH Sacred Scripture, God enters into communion with us, he allows us to cooperate.

⁓

The communion of the Church is the living subject of Scripture. However, here too the principal subject is the Lord himself, who continues to speak through the Scriptures that we have in our hands. I think that we should learn to do three things: to read it in a personal colloquium with the Lord; to read it with the guidance of teachers who have the experience of faith, who have penetrated Sacred Scripture; and to read it in the great company of the Church, in whose liturgy these events never cease to become present anew and in which the Lord speaks with us today.

⁓

One must not read Sacred Scripture as one reads any kind of historical book, such as, for example,

Homer, Ovid or Horace; it is necessary truly to read it as the Word of God, that is, entering into a conversation with God. One must start by praying and talking to the Lord: "Open the door to me." One should not read Scripture in an academic way, but with prayer, saying to the Lord: "Help me to understand your Word, what it is that you want to tell me in this passage."

I urge you to become familiar with the Bible and to have it at hand so that it can be your compass pointing out the road to follow. By reading it, you will learn to know Christ. Note what Saint Jerome said in this regard: "Ignorance of the Scriptures is ignorance of Christ." A time-honored way to study and savor the word of God is *lectio divina*, which constitutes a real and veritable spiritual journey marked out in stages. After the *lectio*, which consists of reading and rereading a passage from Sacred Scripture and taking in the main elements, we proceed to *meditatio*. This is a moment of interior reflection, in which the soul turns to God and tries to understand what his word is saying to us today. Then comes *oratio*, in which we linger to talk with God directly. Finally we come to *contemplatio*. This helps us to keep our hearts attentive to the presence of Christ. Reading, study and meditation of the Word should then flow into a life of consistent fidelity to Christ and his teachings.

It is necessary to take seriously the injunction to consider the word of God to be an indispensable "weapon" in the spiritual struggle. This will be effective and show results if we learn to *listen* to it and then to *obey* it.

Sacred Scripture introduces one into communion with the family of God. Thus, one should not read Sacred Scripture on one's own. Of course, it is always important to read the Bible in a very personal way, in a personal conversation with God; but at the same time, it is important to read it in the company of people with whom one can advance, letting oneself be helped by the great masters of *lectio divina*. These teachers help us to understand better and also to learn how to interpret Sacred Scripture properly. Moreover, it is also appropriate in general to read it in the company of friends who are journeying with me, who are seeking, together with me, how to live with Christ, to find what life the Word of God brings us.

SECULARISM
—For a healthy secularism

A HEALTHY secularism of the State, which does not exclude those ethical references that are ultimately founded in religion, is legitimate.

SEX
—A matter of responsibility

EROS, reduced to pure "sex", has become a commodity, a mere "thing" to be bought and sold, or rather, man himself becomes a commodity.

SIMPLICITY
—Opening oneself to others

BECOMING simpler: this seems to me to be a very beautiful program. Let us seek to put it into practice, and thus we will be more open to the Lord and to people.

SOCIETY AND PUBLIC DEBATE
—Enlightening consciences

IT MUST not be forgotten that, when Churches or Ecclesial Communities intervene in public debate, expressing reservations or recalling various principles, this does not constitute a form of intolerance or an interference, since such interventions are aimed solely at enlightening consciences, enabling them to act freely and responsibly according to the true demands of justice, even when this should conflict with situations of power and personal interest.

Why should there be this lack of understanding in a society where everyone is seeking to understand one another, where communication is everything and where the transparency of all things to all people is the supreme law? The answer lies in the fact that we see the change in our own world and do not sufficiently live that element which binds us all together, the element of our nature as creatures which becomes accessible and becomes reality in a certain history: the history of Christ, who is not against our nature as creatures but restores all that the Creator desired.

SOCIETY

—The "yes" to life

A SOCIETY which forgets God, excludes God, precisely in order to have life, falls into a culture of death. Precisely in order to have life, a "no" is said to the child, because it takes some part of my life away from me; a "no" is said to the future, in order to have the whole of the present; a "no" is said to unborn life as well as to suffering life that is approaching death. What seems to be a culture of life becomes the anticulture of death, where God is absent, where that God who does not ordain hatred but overcomes hatred is absent. Here we truly opt for life. Consequently, everything is connected: the deepest option for the Crucified Christ with the most complete option for life, from the very first moment until the very last.

Family members each live in a world of their own: they are isolated in their thoughts and feelings, which are not united. The great problem of this time—in which each person, desiring to have life for himself, loses it because he is isolated and isolates the other from him—is to rediscover the deep communion which in the end can stem only from a foundation that is common to all souls, from the divine presence that unites all of us.

It is necessary to go to the very fringes of society to take to everyone the light of Christ's message about the meaning of life, the family and society, reaching out to those who live in the desert of neglect and poverty and loving them with the love of the Risen Christ. In every apostolate and in Gospel proclamation, as Saint Paul says, "If I . . . have not love, I am nothing."

SUNDAY
—The Lord's Day

SUNDAY was created because the Lord was raised and entered the community of the Apostles to be with them. And thus, they also understood that Saturday was no longer the liturgical day, but Sunday, on which the Lord wants to be with us physically again and again and wants to nourish us with his Body, so that we ourselves may become his Body in the world.

SUFFERING

—The gift of oneself

My deep personal sharing in the needs and sufferings of others becomes a sharing of my very self with them: if my gift is not to prove a source of humiliation, I must give to others not only something that is my own, but my very self; I must be personally present in my gift.

In sacrificing himself for us all, Christ gave a new meaning to suffering, opening up a new dimension, a new order: the order of love. . . .

SYMBOLS

—The Cross, our shield

THE FIRST gesture of Christians: the Sign of the Cross, which is given to us as a shield that must protect us.

All three characteristics announced by the Prophet—poverty, peace, universality—are summed up in the Sign of the Cross. There was a time—and it has not yet been completely surmounted—in which Christianity was rejected precisely because of the Cross. The Cross speaks of sacrifice, it was said, the Cross is the sign of the denial of life. Instead, we want life in its entirety, without restrictions and without sacrifices. We want to live, all we want is to live. Let us not allow ourselves to be limited by precepts and prohibitions; we want richness and fullness. All this sounds convincing and seductive; it is the language of the serpent that says to us: "Do not be afraid! Quietly eat the fruit of all the trees in the garden!" However, the true, great "Yes" to life is precisely the Cross, the true tree of life.

⁘

The Catholic Church remains convinced that to encourage peace and understanding between peoples and people, it is urgently necessary that religions and their symbols be respected and that believers not be the object of provocations that wound their outlook and religious sentiments. However, intolerance and violence as a response to offenses can never be justified, for this type of response is incompatible with the sacred principles of religion; consequently, we cannot but deplore the actions of those who deliberately exploit the offense caused to religious sentiments to stir up acts of violence, especially since such action is contrary to religion. For believers, as for all people of good will, the only path that leads to peace and brotherhood is that of respect for the religious convictions and practices of others, so that the practice of the religion a person has freely chosen may be guaranteed to each one.

T

TERRORISM
—*God will call to account*

THE FRUITS of faith in God do not consist in devastating forms of antagonism. God, the Creator and Father of all, will call to an even more severe account all those who shed their brother's blood in his name.

TRANSFIGURATION
—*A foretaste of the happiness of Paradise*

WHEN ONE has the grace to live a strong experience of God, it is as if one is living an experience similar to that of the disciples during the Transfiguration: a momentary foretaste of what will constitute the happiness of Paradise. These are usually brief experiences that are sometimes granted by God, especially prior to difficult trials.

TRUTH

—Trust in God

THE DESIRE for the truth is part of human nature itself. The whole of creation is an immense invitation to seek those responses that open human reason to the great response that it has always sought and awaited: The truth of Christian Revelation, found in Jesus of Nazareth, enables anyone to embrace the "mystery" of his own life. As absolute truth, it summons human beings to be open to the transcendent, while respecting both their autonomy as creatures and their freedom. At this point, the relationship between freedom and truth is complete, and we understand the full meaning of the Lord's words: "You will know the truth, and the truth will make you free."

Unless man trusts in God, he trusts in deceit rather than in truth and thereby sinks with his life into emptiness, into death.

Commitment to truth is the soul of justice.

U

UNION
—Belonging to Christ

UNION WITH CHRIST is also union with all those to whom he gives himself. I cannot possess Christ just for myself; I can belong to him only in union with all those who have become, or who will become, his own. Communion draws me out of myself towards him, and thus also towards unity with all Christians. We become "one body", completely joined in a single existence.

UNITY
—Raising our eyes to God

THE CHURCH with her Catholic unity is the great factor that unites in dispersion. In many situations the Church has remained the one reality that functions and makes life continue, that provides the necessary assistance, guarantees coexistence and helps to find the possibility of creating one great solution.

Saint Paul says that divisions are necessary for a certain time and that the Lord knows why: to test us, to train us, to develop us, to make us more humble. But at the same time, we are obliged to move toward unity, and moving toward unity is already a form of unity.

The *unity* of men and women in their multiplicity has become possible because God, this one God of Heaven and earth, has shown himself to us; because the essential truth about our lives, our "where from?" and "where to?" became visible when he revealed himself to us and enabled us to see his face, himself, in Jesus Christ. This truth about the essence of our being, living and dying, a truth that God made visible, unites us and makes us brothers. *Catholicity* and *unity* go hand in hand. And unity has a content: the faith that the Apostles passed on to us in Christ's name.

Catholicity means *universality*—a multiplicity that becomes unity; a unity that nevertheless remains multiplicity. From Paul's words on the Church's universality we have already seen that the ability of nations to get the better of themselves in order to look toward the one God is part of this *unity*. In the second century, the founder of Catholic theology, Saint Irenaeus of Lyons, described very beautifully this bond between catholicity and unity, and I quote him. He says: "The Church spread across the world diligently safeguards this doctrine and this faith, forming as it were one family."

Catholicity does not express only a horizontal dimension, the gathering of many people in unity, but also a vertical dimension: it is only by raising our eyes to God, by opening ourselves to him, that we can truly become one.

V

VOICES OF HEAVEN
—The singing of Angels, voices of God

TRADITION has always claimed that the Angels did not simply speak like people but sang and that their song was of such heavenly beauty that it revealed the beauty of Heaven. Tradition also claims that choirs of treble voices can enable us to hear an echo of the Angels' singing. And it is true that in the singing at the important Liturgies we can sense the presence of the heavenly Liturgy, we can feel a little of the beauty through which the Lord wants to communicate his joy to us.

W

WADOWICE
—In the footsteps of my Predecessor

JOHN PAUL II, returning to his beginnings, often referred to a sign: that of the baptismal font, to which he himself gave special veneration in the Church of Wadowice. In 1979, during his first Pilgrimage in Poland, he stated, "In this baptismal font, on 20 June 1920, I was given the grace to become a son of God, together with faith in my Redeemer, and I was welcomed into the community of the Church." It seems that in these words of John Paul II is contained the key to understanding the consistency of his faith, the radicalism of his Christian life and the desire for sanctity that he continuously manifested. Here is the profound awareness of divine grace, the unconditional love of God for man, that by means of water and the Holy Spirit places the catechumen among the multitude of his children, who are redeemed by the Blood of Christ.

WISDOM
—*All for Christ*

GOD OFFERS US a complete vision of man in history: fascinated by Wisdom, he seeks it and finds it in Christ, leaving everything for him and receiving in exchange the priceless gift of the Kingdom of God; and clothed in temperance, prudence, justice and strength—the "cardinal" virtues—he lives the witness of charity in the Church.

The Gospel wisdom, contained in the writings of the great saints and attested to in their lives, must be brought in a mature way, not childishly or aggressively, to the world of culture and work, to the world of the media and politics, to the world of family and social life.

WOMEN
—*The essential contribution of women*

THE CHURCH has a great debt of gratitude to women. And women do so much for the government of the Church, starting with women Religious, with the sisters of the great Fathers of the Church such as Saint Ambrose, to the great women of the Middle Ages—Saint Hildegard, Saint Catherine of Siena, then Saint Teresa of Avila—and lastly, Mother Teresa. How could we imagine the government of the Church without this contribution, which sometimes becomes very visible, such as when Saint Hildegard criticized the Bishops or when Saint Bridget offered recommendations and Saint Catherine of Siena obtained the return of the Popes to Rome? It has always been a crucial factor without which the Church cannot survive.

WORK
—*The human dimension*

THE PERSON is the "measure of the dignity of work", according to the *Compendium of the Social Doctrine of the Church*. For this reason, the Magisterium has always recalled the human dimension of the activity of work and has redirected it to its true aim, without forgetting that the biblical teaching on work culminates in the commandment to rest. To require, therefore, that Sunday should not be equated to all other days of the week is a civilized decision. Then comes the priority of being over having: this hierarchy of priorities shows clearly that the work environment is fully part of the anthropological issue.

Today, a new and unheard of implication of the social question connected with the protection of life is emerging in this area. We live in a time in which science and technology offer extraordinary possibilities for improving everyone's existence. But a distorted use of this power can seriously and irreparably threaten the destiny of life itself.

WORK OF CHRIST
—All Christ's work is a labor of love

To CONSOLE the Apostles, Christ explains the meaning of his departure: he will go, but he will return; meanwhile, he will not abandon them, will not leave them orphans. He will send the Consoler, the Spirit of the Father, and the Spirit will enable them to understand that Christ's work is a work of love: love of the One who gave himself, love of the Father who has given him.

WORK OF MAN
—The commandment of rest

WORK is of fundamental importance to the fulfillment of the human being and to the development of society. Thus, it must always be organized and carried out with full respect for human dignity and must always serve the common good. At the same time, it is indispensable that people not allow themselves to be enslaved by work or to idolize it, claiming to find in it the ultimate and definitive meaning of life.

"Remember to keep holy the Sabbath day. Six days you may labor and do all your work, but the seventh day is the Sabbath of the Lord, your God." The Sabbath is a holy day, that is, a day consecrated to God on which man understands better the meaning of his life and his work. It can therefore be said that the biblical teaching on work is crowned by the commandment of rest.

WORSHIP
—Worship alone sets us free

WORSHIP alone sets us truly free; worship alone gives us the criteria for our action. Precisely in a world in which guiding criteria are absent and the threat exists that each person will be a law unto himself, it is fundamentally necessary to emphasize worship.

Y

YOUTH

—*A program of love and life*

To BUILD your life on Christ, to accept the word with joy and put its teachings into practice: this, young people of the third millennium, should be your program! There is an urgent need for the emergence of a new generation of apostles anchored firmly in the word of Christ, capable of responding to the challenges of our times and prepared to spread the Gospel far and wide. It is this that the Lord asks of you, it is to this that the Church invites you, and it is this that the world—even though it may not be aware of it—expects of you! If Jesus calls you, do not be afraid to respond to him with generosity, especially when he asks you to follow him in the consecrated life or in the priesthood. Do not be afraid; trust in him and you will not be disappointed.

It is especially adolescents and young people who feel within them the pressing call to love, who need to be freed from the widespread prejudice that Christianity, with its commandments and prohibitions, sets too many obstacles in the path of the joy of love and, in particular, prevents people from fully enjoying the happiness that men and women find in their love for one another. On the contrary, Christian faith and ethics do not wish to stifle love but to make it healthy, strong and truly free: this is the exact meaning of the Ten Commandments, which are not a series of "noes" but a great "yes" to love and to life. Human love, in fact, needs to be purified, to mature and also to surpass itself if it is to be able to become fully human, to be the beginning of true and lasting joy, to respond, that is, to the question of eternity that it bears within it and that it cannot renounce without betraying itself. This is the principal reason why love between a man and a woman is completely fulfilled only in marriage.

Z

ZEAL

—At the service of faith, at the service of life

ON THE Way of the Cross, Paul found the zeal of his faith and kindled the light of love.

⁂

We need well-trained and courageous priests who are free from ambition and fear but convinced of the Gospel Truth, whose chief concern is to proclaim Christ and who are prepared to stoop down to suffering humanity in his Name, enabling everyone, particularly the poor and all who are in difficulty, to experience the comfort of God's love and the warmth of the ecclesial family. This requires human maturity and persevering adherence to the revealed truth; this entails a serious commitment to personal holiness: this is apostolic zeal.

⁂

Zeal and energy must be placed at the service of the protection of human life: all measures that can sustain young couples in forming a family, and the family itself, in the procreation and education of children, are as expedient as ever.

A Short Biography of Pope Benedict XVI

From Christian Bavaria to the Chair of the Apostle Peter:
A collaborator in truth

Joseph Ratzinger, who was elected Pope on April 19, 2005, and took the name of Benedict XVI, was born at Marktl-am-Inn, in the Diocese of Passau, Germany, on April 16, 1927. His father, a policeman, came from a farming family in Lower Bavaria. His mother was the daughter of artisans from Rimsting on Lake Chiem. He spent his childhood and adolescence in Traunstein, a small town near the Austrian border, not far from Salzburg. It is in this context, which he refers to as "Mozartian" because he is a pianist and a music lover, that he received his Christian, human and cultural formation. The faith and education he received at home prepared him for the harsh experience of the Nazi regime and the climate of strong hostility to the Catholic Church. However, it was precisely through this complex situation that he discovered the beauty of faith in Christ. During the last months of the tragedy of World War II, he was enrolled in the auxiliary anti-aircraft corps.

From 1946 to 1951, he studied philosophy and

theology at the Higher School of Philosophy and Theology at Freising and at the University of Munich.

He was ordained a priest on June 29, 1951.

Barely a year later, he began his teaching career at the same school in Freising at which he had studied. In 1953, he earned a doctorate in theology; and in 1957, he qualified as a professor. After having been a teacher of dogma and fundamental theology at Freising, he pursued his teaching career in Bonn (1959–1963), Münster (1963–1966) and Tübingen (1966–1969). From 1969, he was Professor of dogmatics and the history of dogma at the University of Regensburg, where he was also Vice-President of the University. His intense academic activity led him to take on important positions in the German Bishop's Conference and in the International Theological Commission. We should also emphasize his role in the Second Vatican Council as an "expert", which he experienced as a confirmation of his vocation, which he himself has described as "theological".

On March 25, 1977, Pope Paul VI appointed him Archbishop of Munich and Freising. On May 28 that same year he received episcopal ordination. He chose as his episcopal motto: "*Cooperatores veritatis*" (collaborators in truth).

It was also Pope Paul VI who created him a Cardinal, with the title of "Santa Maria Consolatrice al Tiburtino", during the Consistory of June 27, 1977.

On November 25, 1981, John Paul II appointed him Prefect of the Congregation for the Doctrine of the Faith. At the same time he became President of the Pontifical Biblical Commission and of the International Theological Commission and, a few years later, President of the Preparatory Commission for the Catechism of the Catholic Church.

On April 5, 1993, he was called within the College of Cardinals to join the Order of Bishops and took possession of the title of the Suburbicarian See of Velletri-Segni. On November 6, 1998, he was appointed Vice-Dean of the College of Cardinals; and on November 30, 2002, he became its dean: in this capacity, he was entrusted with the Suburbicarian See of Ostia.

Before his election to the Chair of Peter, he was a member of the Council of the Section for Relations with States of the Secretariat of State and of the Congregations for the Oriental Churches; for Divine Worship and the Discipline of the Sacraments; for Bishops; for the Evangelization of Peoples; for Catholic Education; of the Pontifical Council for Promoting Christian Unity; of the

Pontifical Commission for Latin America; and of the Pontifical Commission "Ecclesia Dei".

Pope Benedict XVI's first Encyclical, *Deus Caritas Est* (December 25, 2005), addresses Christian love. Among his numerous and prestigious publications, we note *Introduction to Christianity* (1969, 2004), *The Ratzinger Report* (1985), *Principles of Catholic Theology* (1987), *The Nature and Mission of Theology* (1995), *Salt of the Earth* (1997), *Milestones* (1998), *Spirit of the Liturgy* (2000) and *Truth or Tolerance* (2004), all available in English from Ignatius Press. Also, *Pilgrim Fellowship of Faith: The Church as Communion* (2005), edited by Stephan Otto Horn and Vinzenz Pfnür, contains a helpful bibliography.

Sources

PAGE

11   (1) Address to the Participants in a Seminar Orga-
       nized by the Congregation for Catholic Educa-
       tion (April 1, 2006).
    (2) Ibid.

12   (1) General Audience (November 9, 2005).

13   (1) Homily, Mass on the Feast of the Baptism of
       the Lord, St. Peter's Basilica (January 8, 2006).
    (2) Reflections before the Angelus (July 10, 2005).

15   (1) *Deus Caritas Est*, no. 31. English translation:
       Pope Benedict XVI, *God Is Love* (San Francisco:
       Ignatius Press, 2006).
    (2) Ibid.
    (3) Address to the Clergy of Rome (March 2,
       2006).

16   (1) Homily, Mass for All Workers (March 19, 2006).
    (2) Homily, Mass on the Solemnity of Pentecost
       (June 4, 2006).

17   (1) Address to the Participants in the Ecclesial Con-
       vention of the Diocese of Rome (June 5, 2006).

18   (1) Letter to Cardinal Jean-Louis Tauran on the
       Occasion of the Colloquium "Culture, Reason
       and Freedom", Organized by UNESCO (May
       24, 2005).

As in the original French edition, Scripture references have been omitted from the citations, and ellipses were not used to indicate such omissions.

19 (1) Homily, Mass on the Fourth Sunday of Advent at the Roman Parish of Santa Maria Consolatrice (December 18, 2005).

(2) Address to the Participants in the Plenary Assembly of the Pontifical Council for Migrants and Itinerant People (May 15, 2006).

20 (1) Ibid.

(2) Ibid.

22 (1) Address to the Clergy of Rome (March 2, 2006).

(2) Reflection before the Angelus (June 19, 2005).

(3) Address at the Meeting with the Youth of Rome and Lazio (April 6, 2006).

24 (1) Address to the Clergy of Rome (March 2, 2006).

(2) Ibid.

25 (1) Ibid.

(2) Address to President Ciampi of the Italian Republic, Official Visit to the Quirinal Palace (June 24, 2005).

(3) Address to the Clergy of Rome (March 2, 2006).

26 (1) General Audience (June 8, 2005).

(2) General Audience (June 15, 2005).

27 (1) Address to the Diplomatic Corps Accredited to the Holy See (January 9, 2006).

(2) Message for the 21st World Youth Day (February 22, 2006 [Celebrated on April 9]).

28 (1) Reflection before the Angelus (January 1, 2006).

(2) Address at the Meeting with the Youth of Rome and Lazio (April 6, 2006).

30 (1) Address to the Participants in the Ecclesial Convention of the Diocese of Rome (June 5, 2006).
(2) *Deus Caritas Est*, no. 16.
(3) Reflection before the Angelus, Second Sunday of Lent (March 12, 2006).

31 (1) *Deus Caritas Est*, no. 31.
(2) Address to the Parish Priests of the Diocese of Aosta (July 25, 2005).

32 (1) Ibid.
(2) Homily, Mass for the Lord's Supper (April 13, 2006).
(3) Address at the Meeting with the Youth of Rome and Lazio (April 6, 2006).

33 (1) Ibid.

34 (1) Homily, Mass for the Lord's Supper (April 13, 2006).
(2) Message for the 43rd World Day of Prayer for Vocations, Sunday, May 7 (dated March 5, 2006; released March 30, 2006).

35 (1) Reflection before Regina Caeli (June 4, 2006).
(2) Homily Given at Ephesus (November 29, 2006).
(3) General Audience (November 23, 2005).

37 (1) Address after the Way of the Cross at the Colosseum, Good Friday (April 14, 2006).

39 (1) Homily, Mass on the Solemnity of Pentecost (June 4, 2006).

40 (1) Address to the Members of the Pontifical Bibli-
        cal Commission on the Occasion of Their Ple-
        nary Assembly (April 27, 2006).
    (2) Address to the Participants in the Plenary As-
        sembly of the Congregation for the Doctrine of
        the Faith (February 10, 2006).
    (3) Reflection before the Angelus (March 19,
        2006).

41 (1) Ibid.

42 (1) Address to the Italian Branch (UCID) of the
        International Christian Union of Business Ex-
        ecutives (March 4, 2006).
    (2) Ibid.

43 (1) Address to the Members of the Pontifical Bibli-
        cal Commission on the Occasion of Their Ple-
        nary Assembly (April 27, 2006).
    (2) Homily, Mass for All Workers (March 19,
        2006).
    (3) Address to the Clergy of Rome and Lazio
        (March 2, 2006).

44 (1) Address to the Members of the European Popu-
        lar Party on the Occasion of the Organization's
        Study Days on Europe (March 30, 2006).
    (2) Ibid.

45 (1) *Deus Caritas Est*, no. 1.
    (2) *Deus Caritas Est*, no. 2.

46 (1) *Deus Caritas Est*, no. 10.
    (2) *Deus Caritas Est*, no. 2.
    (3) *Deus Caritas Est*, no. 12.

47 (1) *Deus Caritas Est*, no. 5.
  (2) *Deus Caritas Est*, no. 6.
  (3) *Deus Caritas Est*, no. 4.
  (4) *Deus Caritas Est*, no. 1.

48 (1) Homily, Mass for Baptism of 10 Infants, St. Peter's (January 8, 2006).
  (2) *Deus Caritas Est*, no. 16.
  (3) Homily, Mass on the Solemnity of the Annunciation (March 25, 2006).
  (4) Address to the Parish Priests of the Diocese of Aosta (July 25, 2005).
  (5) Address to Members of John Paul II Institute for Studies on Marriage and the Family (May 11, 2006).
  (6) *Deus Caritas Est*, no. 18.

49 (1) *Deus Caritas Est*, no. 17.

50 (1) Address at the Meeting with the Youth of Rome and Lazio (April 6, 2006).
  (2) Address to the Members of John Paul II Institute for Studies on Marriage and the Family (May 11, 2006).

51 (1) Address to the Participants in the Ecclesial Convention of the Diocese of Rome (June 5, 2006).
  (2) Address to the Members of the John Paul II Institute for Studies on Marriage and the Family (May 11, 2006).
  (3) Letter to Cardinal Alfonso López Trujillo, President of the Pontifical Council of the Family, Prior to the Fifth World Meeting of Families (May 17, 2005).
  (4) Ibid.

52 (1) Address at the Meeting with the Youth of Rome and Lazio (April 6, 2006).
  (2) Address to the Members of the John Paul II Institute for Studies on Marriage and the Family (May 11, 2006).
  (3) Address at the Meeting with the Youth of Rome and Lazio (April 6, 2006).

53 (1) Reflection before the Angelus (December 26, 2005).
  (2) *Deus Caritas Est*, no. 41.
  (3) Ibid.
  (4) Homily, Mass on the Solemnity of the Annunciation (March 25, 2006).

54 (1) Address to a Group of Bishops from Poland on Their *Ad Limina* Visit (November 26, 2005).

55 (1) Christmas Address to the Roman Curia (December 22, 2005).

56 (1) Address to the Members of the Pontifical Biblical Commission on the Occasion of Their Plenary Assembly (April 27, 2006).
  (2) *Deus Caritas Est*, no. 15.

57 (1) Address to the Roman Clergy (March 2, 2006).

58 (1) At the Recitation of the Rosary (January 5, 2006).
  (2) Reflection before the Angelus, World Day of Peace (January 1, 2006).
  (3) Ibid.
  (4) Homily, Mass, The World Day of Peace (January 1, 2006).

59 (1) Address to the Diplomatic Corps Accredited to the Holy See (January 9, 2006).
    (2) Homily, Mass, The World Day of Peace (January 1, 2006).

60 (1) *Deus Caritas Est*, no. 37.
    (2) General Audience (June 22, 2005).
    (3) *Deus Caritas Est*, no. 36.

61 (1) Homily, Mass on the Solemnity of the Assumption of the Blessed Virgin Mary into Heaven (August 15, 2005).

62 (1) Homily, Mass on the Solemnity of the Annunciation (March 25, 2006).

63 (1) Address at the Meeting with the Youth of Rome and Lazio (April 6, 2006).
    (2) *Deus Caritas Est*, no. 38.

64 (1) Address to Canadian Bishops on an *Ad Limina* Visit (September 8, 2006).
    (2) Address to the Writers of the College of *La Civiltà Cattolica* (February 17, 2006).

66 (1) Address to the Clergy of Rome (March 2, 2006).
    (2) Address at the Meeting with the Youth of Rome and Lazio (April 6, 2006).
    (3) Ibid.

67 (1) Ibid.

68 (1) Message for the 21st World Youth Day (February 22, 2006; celebrated on April 9).
    (2) Address at the Meeting with the Youth of Rome and Lazio (April 6, 2006).

69 (1) Address to President Ciampi of the Italian Republic, Official Visit to the Quirinal Palace (June 24, 2005).

(2) *Deus Caritas Est*, no. 5.

(3) Address to the Clergy of Rome (March 2, 2006).

70 (1) Address to the Members of the European Popular Party on the Occasion of the Organization's Study Days on Europe (March 30, 2006).

(2) Address to the Clergy of Rome (March 2, 2006).

71 (1) Ibid.

(2) Ibid.

72 (1) Address to Pilgrims from Madrid (July 4, 2006).

(2) Address to the Parish Priests of the Diocese of Aosta (July 25, 2005).

73 (1) *Deus Caritas Est*, no. 34.

(2) Christmas Address to the Roman Curia (December 22, 2005).

(3) Homily, Mass on the Feast of the Baptism of the Lord, St. Peter's Basilica (January 8, 2006).

(4) Homily, Mass on Palm Sunday (April 9, 2006).

74 (1) Address to the Ambassador of Morocco Accredited to the Holy See (February 20, 2006).

76 (1) Reflection before the Angelus (February 26, 2006).

(2) Reflection before the Angelus (March 12, 2006).

77 (1) Address to the Participants in the Plenary Assembly of the Congregation for the Doctrine of the Faith (February 10, 2006).

(2) Homily, Mass, The Immaculate Conception (December 8, 2005).

(3) Address to the Diplomatic Corps Accredited to the Holy See (January 9, 2006).

78 (1) *Deus Caritas Est*, no. 14.

(2) Address to the Clergy of Rome (March 2, 2006).

79 (1) Ibid.

(2) Homily, Mass on the Solemnity of SS. Peter and Paul (June 29, 2005).

(3) Ibid.

80 (1) Ibid.

81 (1) Address to the Sistine Chapel Choir (December 20, 2006).

82 (1) Apostolic Visit to Poland, Greeting at the Meeting with the People, Rynek Square, Wadowice (May 27, 2006).

83 (1) Homily, Mass for the 500th Anniversary of the Swiss Guards (May 6, 2006).

(2) Apostolic Visit to Poland, Address at the Encounter with Men and Women Religious, Seminarians and Representatives of Ecclesial Movements, Czestochowa (May 26, 2006).

(3) Address to the Clergy of Rome (March 2, 2006).

84 (1) Address to the Members of the Italian Christian Workers Associations (January 27, 2006).

85 (1) Homily, Mass on the Solemnity of Pentecost (June 4, 2006).

(2) Homily, Mass for All Workers (March 19, 2006).

86 (1) Ibid.
   (2) Christmas Address to the Roman Curia (December 22, 2005).

87 (1) Message for the 21st World Youth Day (February 22, 2006 [Celebrated on April 9]).
   (2) Address to the Participants in the Ecclesial Convention of the Diocese of Rome (June 5, 2006).

89 (1) Address after the Way of the Cross at the Colosseum, Good Friday (April 14, 2006).
   (2) Address to the Community of the "Almo Collegio Caranica" (January 20, 2006).
   (3) Address to political authorities of Rome and Lazio, January 12, 2007.